D1493538

SCOTTISH

AND PROUD OF IT

GREIG FINDLAY

summersdale

SCOTTISH AND PROUD OF IT

Summersdale Publishers Ltd
46 West Street
Chichester
West Sussex
PO19 1RP
UK

www.summersdale.com

Printed and bound in the Czech Republic

ISBN: 978-1-84953- 523-6

Substantial discounts on bulk quantities of Summersdale books are available to corporations, professional associations and other organisations. For details contact Nicky Douglas by telephone: +44 (0) 1243 756902, fax: +44 (0) 1243 786300 or email: nicky@summersdale.com.

CONTENTS

INTRODUCTION

From the awe-inspiring islands of Shetland down to the ditches of the Antonine Wall, perhaps stopping off en route for a few holes at the famous St Andrews golf course or pausing to consider how the sci-fi-fantastic Falkirk Wheel works, this little book will take you on a tour of everything that makes this great country unique.

From Scotland's deep thinkers to its deep-fried Mars Bars, from its brilliant biologists to its caber tossers and some of the world's most celebrated icons of sport and film, we will gaze in awe at the achievements of its people. Come and join us on a magical journey through the land of haggis, Highlands and Hogmanay and discover what makes people Scottish… and proud of it!

MAKING HISTORY

IMPORTANT DATES
IN OUR HISTORY

Held annually every first Saturday of
September (since around 900 years ago),
the famous and iconic **Braemar Gathering**
is one of the events known globally as
Highland Games. The Games celebrate
Gaelic cultural pastimes emblematic of
Scotland's ancient history – most famously,
the world-renowned caber toss. A caber
is made from a larch tree and is usually
19 feet tall and weighs around 175 pounds.
How far do you think you could throw one?

It was on **11 September 1297** that the iconic Battle of Stirling Bridge, fought during Scotland's first War of Independence, took place and marked an astounding victory against great odds for the Scots, led by William Wallace and Andrew de Moray. Today, visitors to Stirling's Wallace Monument can see the broadsword it is believed Wallace used during the battle.

In **June 1314**, the bloody Battle of Bannockburn was fought. This historic conflict saw the English army, led by Edward II, defeated by the forces of Robert the Bruce (then 'King of the Scots'), again during the First War of Scottish Independence. On the first day of the battle, Robert the Bruce delivered a fatal blow to the English knight Henry de Bohun and went on to ultimately win a decisive victory for Scotland.

The Declaration of Arbroath, signed on **6 April 1320** and addressed to Pope John XXII, is a famous document in Scottish history and an eloquent expression of a proud Scottish nationhood. Believed to have been written by the Chancellor of Scotland, Bernard of Kilwinning, the letter outlined the country's status as an independent sovereign state that had the right to defend itself if invaded.

It is not for glory or riches or honours that we fight, But only for liberty, which no good man will consent to lose but with his life.

THE DECLARATION OF ARBROATH

On **17 July 1695** the Bank of Scotland was created with the intent of supporting Scottish businesses. It became the first bank in the world to print its own banknotes, and still continues to do so. The Bank of Scotland is the second-oldest surviving bank in the UK and, during the middle of the eighteenth century, it had a long-running rivalry with The Royal Bank of Scotland. Each bank wanted to put the other out of business but after twenty-odd years of disagreement they decided to call a truce in 1751 when the banks finally agreed to accept each other's notes!

England had absorbed Wales and Cornwall by 1543 but it was not until the Acts of Union were passed in **1707** that the English and Scottish parliaments became one to form a united kingdom. Though proposed a century earlier, the Act did not take effect until 1707 due to the mistrust and suspicion of both countries. When the treaty was finally signed, Scotland benefited from an increase in trade opportunities but still maintained its proud non-English identity.

We look to Scotland for all our ideas of civilisation.

VOLTAIRE

In **1964**, the massive Forth Road Bridge was officially completed alongside the iconic rail bridge, instantly becoming the main road artery connecting the north and south of the country and transforming its transport links. Each of the bridge's main cables is comprised of 11,618 steel wires twisted together by a process called 'cable-spinning', an engineering first of its kind in Europe. Laid end to end, the total length of wire would wrap around the earth one and a quarter times.

Following a referendum in 1997, Scotland regained its parliamentary independence through the Scotland Act **1998**, which established a devolved Scottish Parliament separate from that of Great Britain. For the first time in 291 years Scotland could pass, amend and repeal its own legislature. Even though the powers of the Scottish parliament were limited, and many areas of lawmaking are still controlled by the Houses of Parliament in London, this was still a very important milestone in Scottish political history.

Every **30 November** the people of Scotland unite to celebrate their patron saint, St Andrew. Since 2006, St Andrew's Day has been a national bank holiday and a day of feasting and patriotic celebrations. St Andrew was one of the twelve apostles and one of the first followers of Jesus Christ. The diagonal cross, or 'saltire', as it is known, on the Scottish flag originates from the cross that St Andrew was crucified on while spreading the word of Christianity in Greece.

Some may know it as 'New Year's Eve' but in Scotland it is called **Hogmanay**. The wonderful tradition of 'first-footing' is still common and requires that the 'first foot' to step into the house after midnight on Hogmanay should ideally belong to a tall, dark, handsome stranger bearing coal or whisky, thus ensuring good luck to the household for the rest of the year. Try it out this Hogmanay by meeting as many of the criteria as you can!

On Thursday, **18 September 2014** the citizens of Scotland will be asked one of the most important questions of their lives: should Scotland again become an independent country? The referendum will be historic and a 'yes' vote would have far-reaching consequences. Coincidentally, 2014 also happens to be the year two prestigious sporting events – the Ryder Cup golf tournament and the Commonwealth Games – are being held in Scotland. Not to mention, of course, the 700th anniversary of the Battle of Bannockburn.

I feel a sort of reverence in going over these scenes in this most beautiful country, which I am proud to call my own…

QUEEN VICTORIA

WE CAN BE HEROES

HEROES

PEOPLE WE CAN BE PROUD TO CALL OUR OWN

Proud Scotsman and iconic inventor and engineer, **James Watt** is credited with improving the steam engine in the eighteenth century, improvements that were fundamental in kick-starting the Industrial Revolution through better transportation lines. Now Watt is remembered through the 'watt', a unit of measurement used to describe electrical and mechanical power. Watt also coined the term 'horsepower' as a way of comparing the output of a steam engine to the power of draft horses.

Red MacGregor was known for his deeply red hair. He was also known for being **Rob Roy**, Scotland's eighteenth-century version of the English outlaw Robin Hood. Rob Roy became infamous for his battles with feudal landowners and was thereby considered a folk hero. After his death in 1734, Rob Roy's legend expanded globally. In the 1995 Hollywood movie, *Rob Roy*, the legendary hero was played by the Irish actor Liam Neeson.

Hung, drawn and quartered in most brutal fashion on 23 August 1305, **William Wallace** has since gone down in history as the fiercest warrior, and leader, in the struggle for Scotland's independence. He is remembered mostly for his famous victory over the English at the Battle of Stirling Bridge, where Wallace, it is rumoured, skinned the English knight, Hugh Cressingham, and used his skin as a 'baldrick' – a shoulder pouch in which to carry his sword.

We come here with no peaceful intent, but ready for battle, determined to avenge our wrongs and set our country free. Let your masters come and attack us: we are ready to meet them beard to beard.

WILLIAM WALLACE

Mary, Queen of Scots was one of Scotland's most influential and fascinating monarchs. Mary was just six days old when she became queen of Scotland in 1542. Married by the age of fourteen to the future king of France, she was married again at twenty-three to her cousin, Lord Darnley. Having given birth to James, the next king of Scotland and England, she was allegedly instrumental in Darnley's murder the following year. She subsequently fled to England, whereupon she was arrested by her cousin, Queen Elizabeth I. Ultimately found guilty of a plot to kill Elizabeth, and having been held captive in England for almost nineteen years, she was finally executed in 1587.

Born as the only son of Mary, Queen of Scots, **King James I** was the king of Scotland when, in 1603, he also became the king of England, linking the two crowns for the first time. Named as her successor by Elizabeth I (the queen who killed his mother, let's not forget), James's greatest contribution to the world was to be the King James Bible – one of the first English translations of it.

Nicknamed '**Black Agnes**' for her dark
hair and eyes, Agnes Randolph was a true
Scottish heroine of the fourteenth century.
Famed for the defence of her home,
Dunbar Castle, she resisted the English
forces – led by William Montagu – who
had taken siege over her castle and land.
Refusing to surrender, Agnes (along with
a few servants and guards) defended the
grounds for six months until Montagu
and his men withdrew, sulking no
doubt for having lost a fight to a girl.

For who would leave,
unbrib'd, Hibernia's Land,
Or change the rocks of
Scotland for the Strand?

SAMUEL JOHNSON

Charles Edward Louis John Casimir
Sylvester Severino Maria Stuart was
known after his death, in 1788, simply as
Bonnie Prince Charlie. Also known as
the Young Pretender, he led the Jacobite
Rising in 1745 to win the crowns of
England and Scotland back for his deposed
father, King James III of England and VIII
of Scotland, who had been overthrown
by the Dutch king, William of Orange.
Although he failed in his quest, the
Bonnie Prince's noble endeavours and
bravery have been celebrated down the
centuries, to this day remembered in the
beautiful folk song 'Charlie Is My Darling'.

Flora MacDonald, Scotland's bravest Highland heroine, is not only famous for aiding the escape of Bonnie Prince Charlie following the prince's defeat at the Battle of Culloden in 1746, but also for resisting American loyalists alongside her soldier husband during the American War of Independence, after they had emigrated to North Carolina in 1774. If that wasn't enough, years later on her return voyage home to Scotland, Flora's ship was attacked by a privateer! Refusing to leave the ship's deck as ordered, Flora was wounded in the arm. She died at the age of sixty-eight at her home on the Isle of Skye.

Greyfriars Bobby is Scotland's most iconic dog. The Skye Terrier is revered for his loyalty to his master, Edinburgh policeman John Gray. The legend goes that after his master died, Greyfriars Bobby sat by his grave, protecting it lovingly for fourteen years, until his own death in January 1872. A statue of Bobby now resides at the corner of Edinburgh's Candlemaker Row and George IV Bridge.

Whenever you think of influential Scottish icons, it is **Alexander Graham Bell**'s name that first pops into your head. And for good reason; he is credited with inventing the telephone. Not a lot of people know that Bell's mother and sister were deaf and this situation greatly influenced his desire to invent a device that aided hearing. Interestingly, Bell was not given the middle name Graham at birth – his father gave the name to him as a birthday present when he was eleven!

Alex Ferguson needs no introduction. As manager of the most successful football team *ever*, Manchester United, Fergie's reign over the past quarter-century throws up some unbeatable stats, including thirteen Premier League wins, and two Champions League wins. He managed over 1,500 games, won forty-nine titles in all, and signed some of the most recognisable names in the sport – Beckham, Giggs, Rooney, Scholes and Cantona, to name just a few.

Did not strong connections draw me elsewhere, I believe Scotland would be the country I would choose to end my days in.

BENJAMIN FRANKLIN

SOMETHING TO REMEMBER US BY

OUR NATION'S CULTURAL HIGHLIGHTS

The mark of a Scot of all classes is that he remembers and cherishes the memory of his forebears, good or bad.

ROBERT LOUIS STEVENSON

Think of Scotland and you think of **tartan**. This ancient pattern of woven wool was devised as a way of distinguishing different, and often warring, Scottish clans. Following the repeal in 1782 of the Dress Act of 1746 (which had sought to ban tartan and bring clan culture under government control), tartan was no longer restricted to Highland clan apparel and was adopted as the symbolic national dress of Scotland. Today, Tartan Day is celebrated around the world every 6 April (the date the Declaration of Arbroath was signed in 1320). Coincidentally, when the world's first colour photograph was taken in 1861, it was of a tartan ribbon.

It may not be the oldest university in Scotland (that's equally prestigious St Andrews), but the **University of Edinburgh** (founded in 1583) remains one of the most prestigious in the world. Every year the university receives around 47,000 applications, making it one of the most popular universities in the UK. Its famous alumni include, among many others, Walter Scott, Alexander Fleming, J. M. Barrie, J. K. Rowling and Marcus Mumford.

This nation must rank among the most enlightened in the universe. Politics, religion and literature have made of Scotland something beyond compare…

CHARLES DE RÉMUSAT

Golf has been played on the links site of the **St Andrew's Old Course**, in Fife, for around 600 years, making it one of the oldest golf courses in the world. It's also regarded as the best. Another six courses have been added on the links over the years and now over 230,000 rounds of golf are played across the seven courses each year! The Tom Morris Shop, near the eighteenth hole, is also the oldest golf shop in the world. It opened in 1866.

Loch Ness is renowned for being the largest body of fresh water in Britain; its surface area could hold the population of the world ten times over. Despite the arctic-feeling Scottish temperatures, Loch Ness never freezes over.

The **Cairngorms**, a mountain range in the Highlands of Scotland, are a place of outstanding natural beauty. The Cairngorms region is Britain's largest National Park and takes up 6 per cent of all the land of Scotland. It's big! The Cairngorms are home to fifty-five mountain summits and five of the UK's highest mountains (do you know which ones?) reside in the park.

Not the brother of Sebastian Coe, as many English people believe, **Glen Coe** is an area of myth, legend and history and the iconic resting place of the famous Clan MacDonald. A region of rugged wilderness, Glen Coe is today a hotspot for climbers and skiers, but, in 1692, it was the scene of a massacre. The MacDonald clan had been invited there by King William to be pardoned for their betrayal during the unsuccessful Jacobite Rising. Instead, thirty-eight men, women and children were butchered and another forty died of exposure after their homes were burned.

Built on top of a huge naturally formed crag, with steep cliffs on three sides, **Stirling Castle** is a sight to behold. The castle is one of the largest and most historically important in Scottish history, not least because Robert the Bruce recaptured the castle from the English after the Battle of Bannockburn in 1314. Around 400,000 people visit the castle every year.

Scone Palace, Perthshire, is a place of outstanding historical importance and considered a national treasure due its beautiful natural surroundings and because of its history as the rightful home of the 'Stone of Scone', or 'Stone of Destiny'; an oblong block of sandstone that has been used for centuries in the coronation of all British monarchs. The stone was last used in the coronation of Queen Elizabeth II.

On 24 May 2002, Queen Elizabeth II opened the fascinating **Falkirk Wheel**; the world's first – and only – rotating boat lift. Part of the Millennium Link project designed to regenerate the country's canals, the wheel is 35 metres (115 feet) tall (the height of eight double-decker buses) and cost £17.5 million to build.

Holyrood Palace has been the official Scottish residence of the monarch of Great Britain since the sixteenth century. Founded as an abbey by David, King of Scots in 1128, this significant palace is located at the opposite end to Edinburgh Castle on the famous Royal Mile. Each summer Queen Elizabeth spends just one week at Holyrood, attending to royal engagements.

Bonnie lassie, will ye go,
Will ye go, will ye go,
Bonnie lassie, will ye go
To the birks of Aberfeldie!

SCOTTISH FOLK SONG

STARS IN OUR EYES

THE ENTERTAINERS WE LOVE

Artist **Jack Vettriano** (born Jack Hoggan) was born in Methill, Fife, in 1951. He created one of Britain's best-selling images, 'The Singing Butler', which he painted in 1992, and which set a Scottish record when the original sold for £744,500. Famously, Vettriano only took up painting as a hobby after his girlfriend bought him a set of watercolours on his twenty-first birthday.

Few would disagree that **Sean Connery** is Scotland's finest acting export. He is, in most people's eyes, the definitive James Bond, having played the role in seven films between 1962 and 1983. A former artist's model, milkman, sailor and coffin polisher, Mr Connery is also one of the proudest Scotsmen you'll ever meet.

Scotland should be nothing less than equal with all the other nations of the world.

SEAN CONNERY

Voted regularly as the funniest comedian of all time, and with an accomplished acting career on top, **Billy Connolly** – or the 'Big Yin' as he is known in Scotland – is without doubt a proud Scottish national treasure. In 2001, Glasgow University gave the former shipyard welder an honorary doctorate, turning Mr Connolly into Dr Connolly – not bad for a boy who left school at fifteen.

There are two seasons in Scotland: June and winter.

BILLY CONNOLLY

Formula One racing driver **Jackie Stewart** is as legendary as they come. Nicknamed the 'Flying Scot', Dunbartonshire-born Stewart won three World Drivers' Championships between 1969 and 1973. Knighted in 2001, Stewart is widely considered to be one of the best Formula One drivers of all time.

Stirling-born thoroughbred-horse jockey, **Willie Carson**, was one of the world's best-loved horse riders. He was Champion Jockey five times between 1972 and 1983 and won seventeen British Classic races. In 1990 alone he rode 187 winning horses!

Andy Murray is the Scottish tennis champion who, in 2013, became the first British male in seventy-seven years to win the prestigious Wimbledon Championship. In 2012, he also won gold at the London Olympics tennis tournament, much to the nation's shock and awe! Go Andy!

We Scots have a fierce pride
in the things we do that
others can never appreciate.

ANDY MURRAY

Everybody knows the name **Midge Ure**. In addition to a successful music career with top bands like Ultravox, he was co-organiser (with Bob Geldof) of the first-of-its-kind charity appeal Band Aid (1984), and later Live Aid (2005), which together raised millions around the world to help alleviate the Ethiopian poverty crisis. Ure co-wrote the mammoth-selling Band Aid single 'Do They Know It's Christmas?', a song that made himself, Geldof and their cause household names, and will forever remind us of the power of song in uniting the world.

Annie Lennox is the quintessential Scottish songwriter and performer. Born in Aberdeen, Lennox – along with partner Dave Stewart – wrote many of the eighties' biggest hits under the band name Eurythmics. As a solo performer, Lennox sold millions of copies of her solo albums, starting with *Diva* (1992), and won an Oscar in 2004 for her song 'Into the West', part of the soundtrack for *The Lord of the Rings: The Return of the King*.

Born in Perth in 1971, Scotsman **Ewan McGregor** has played a variety of complex characters that today have made him one of the most in-demand actors on the planet. He was inspired to get into acting by his uncle Denis Lawson, who played pilot Wedge Antilles in the first *Star Wars* movie, and McGregor himself went on to play the vital role of Obi-Wan Kenobi in the prequels to that film over twenty years later!

I'm fiercely proud
to be Scottish.

EWAN MCGREGOR

Hailing from Auchtermuchty in Fife, **The Proclaimers** (Charlie and Craig Reid) became a worldwide singing sensation. Their song 'I'm Gonna Be (500 miles)' was a hit all around the world after it featured in the Johnny Depp movie *Benny & Joon* (1993) and has since featured in countless other movies. It is also played before the start of every Scottish national home football game and their music is the basis of the 2013 musical film, *Sunshine On Leith*.

Edinburgh-born **Ronnie Corbett**, the smaller one of the acclaimed 'Two Ronnies', is one of Britain's most-loved comedy actors. Appearing in *The Frost Report* in the 1960s, 5-foot-1-inch-tall Corbett hit the big time alongside friend and double-act comedy cohort Ronnie Barker in their brilliantly written and performed BBC show, *The Two Ronnies*, from 1971 to 1987.

In August 2012 it was almost impossible to have a conversation in Britain without hearing the name of track cyclist, and undisputed king of London 2012, **Chris Hoy**. Eleven-time world champion and six-time Olympic champion, Edinburgh-born Hoy won his first world title, in 2002, by one-thousandth of a second! Hoy was voted the BBC Sports Personality of the Year in 2008 and was knighted in the 2009 New Year Honours list.

Winner of the British Open in 2009 and
four-time LPGA Tour winner, **Catriona
Matthew** has been the superstar of
Scottish ladies professional golf, winning
eleven major titles in all. Born in Edinburgh,
Matthew became an MBE in 2010, having
hit a work/life balance hole-in-one
when she married her caddy in 2007.

Scotland has an inbuilt sound system that never stops thumping.

KT TUNSTALL

THE WRITE STUFF

STUFF

FAMOUS WRITERS, POETS AND PLAYWRIGHTS

Scotland's most treasured writer, **Robert Burns** is often referred to as its national poet, or simply as 'the Bard', such is the prestigious place he holds in the hearts of the people. Although he died in 1796 at the age of thirty-seven Burns's legacy was rich – over 550 songs and poems, at least twelve children (!), and a vital influence on many of the world's greatest writers and poets over the last two centuries.

O Scotia! my dear,
my native soil!
For whom my warmest
wish to heaven is sent;
Long may thy hardy sons
of rustic toil
Be blest with health, and
peace, and sweet content.

ROBERT BURNS

First published when she was just fifteen, **Carol Ann Duffy** is a Scottish poet and playwright of the highest order, with many of her poems nestled in the school curriculum. The poet herself explains that she 'likes to use simple words in a complicated way,' thereby exercising the minds of thousands of schoolchildren up and down the land. In 2009, Duffy became the first Scot, and first woman, to become Britain's Poet Laureate, succeeding Andrew Motion. Woman's Hour on BBC Radio 4 included Duffy in their chart of the top 100 most powerful women in the UK in 2013.

In 2008 *The Times* voted mainstream-fiction and science-fiction author **Iain Banks** one of the 'Greatest British Writers Since 1945'. His debut novel, the grizzly and warped *The Wasp Factory* (1984), tells the story of sixteen-year-old Frank Cauldhame's childhood and unstable relationship with his father. It is regularly voted one of the top 100 books of the twentieth century.

Chances are you've heard of **James Matthew Barrie** before. He was born in Kirriemuir in 1860 and introduced the world to the beloved characters Peter Pan, Captain Hook, Tinker Bell and the Lost Boys. It's one of the most revered children's books ever written and has sold, so far, over 85 million copies – of which all royalties still go to Great Ormond Street Hospital in London.

The works of Scottish poet, writer and essayist **Robert Louis Stevenson** speak for themselves. *The Strange Case of Dr Jekyll and Mr Hyde (1886)*, *Treasure Island (1883)* and *Kidnapped (1886)*, to name but three, place Stevenson high on the list of Western literature's most important writers. A lesser-known fact is that, in 1891, Stevenson wrote a letter to a twelve-year-old girl, whose birthday fell on Christmas Day, to say he was transferring the legal rights of his birthday over to her –'I have now no further use for a birthday of any description,' he wrote.

Award-winning novelist **Muriel Spark** published her best-known book, *The Prime of Miss Jean Brodie*, in 1961, a story about the titular teacher and her mentoring of six ten-year-old girls at an Edinburgh school. In 2005, the novel was chosen by *Time* magazine as one of the hundred best English-language novels of the twentieth century.

Arthur Conan Doyle's *Sherlock Holmes* – written between 1887 and 1914 – is without doubt his most famous and influential work. Doyle's other era-defining adventure story, *The Lost World* (1912), tells the tale of a South American expedition to where prehistoric animals still roam the land. Sound familiar? That's probably because it has influenced many popular novels and films, including Michael Crichton's *Jurassic Park*. A spruced-up statue of Sherlock Holmes currently stands at Picardy Place, Edinburgh, where the writer was born.

Mole, Ratty, Mr Toad, Mr Badger, Otter, Chief Weasel – despite **Kenneth Grahame**'s lack of imagination when it came to naming his characters, you can't argue with the storytelling imagination on display in *The Wind in the Willows* (1908), a masterpiece of literature from the Edinburgh-born writer. In 2010, a rare first edition of this beloved classic children's tale was sold at auction for £32,400.

Celebrated poet and novelist **Jackie Kay** was born in Edinburgh in 1961 and in 2006 received an MBE for her services to literature. In 1992, Kay won the Scottish First Book of the Year for her book of poetry *The Adoption Papers*. In 1998, she also won the prestigious Guardian Fiction Prize for *Trumpet*, the fascinating story of the American jazz musician, Billy Tipton.

Walter Scott, he of 'Oh, what a tangled web we weave, when first we practise to deceive' fame, was one of the world's most popular nineteenth-century writers and playwrights. Born in Edinburgh in 1771, Scott's legacy remains in classic novels such as *Rob Roy* (1817) and *Ivanhoe* (1820), both of which belong to Scott's 'Waverley novels' series – so-called because, Scott having denied authorship of them for many years, they took their name from *Waverley*, the first book in the series. Edinburgh's impressive, and recently refurbished, Waverley train station is named after Scott's erstwhile pseudonym. The iconic Scott Monument towers nearby.

Land of brown heath
and shaggy wood,
Land of the mountain
and the flood,
Land of my sires!
what mortal hand
Can e'er untie the filial band
That knits me to thy
rugged strand?

WALTER SCOTT

FOOD FOR THOUGHT

OUR LANDMARK DISHES

Cullen skink may sound difficult to swallow, but this famous thick soup of smoked haddock, potatoes and onions, is a speciality from Cullen in Moray. The name comes from the Gaelic word for 'essence', and used to apply to a type of popular broth that contained beef shavings, not fish. However, in the 1890s the people of the north fell on tough times, beef was hard to come by and smoked haddock was substituted. An authentic Cullen skink will use 'Finnan haddie' (Finnan haddock).

My theory is that all
of Scottish cuisine is
based on a dare.

MIKE MYERS

Usually served as the delicious accompaniments to the famous haggis, **neeps and tatties** are the Scottish versions of turnips and potatoes. These two root vegetables are lovingly mashed with buckets of butter and served piping hot. The word 'neeps' is a corruption of 'new turnips', a term once used to distinguish them from the English 'old turnips'. You might also hear neeps referred to as 'tumshies'.

Traditionally eaten on Burns Night (25 January) to commemorate the life of Robert Burns, who addressed one of his poems to it ('Address to a Haggis'), **the haggis** is celebrated across the entire land for its unique flavour, texture and amber colour. For an authentic Scottish recipe, take the heart and lungs of a lamb, mince together with onions, suet, oats, coriander, mace and nutmeg, and spoon into a sheep's stomach, which has been soaked overnight in cold, salted water. Boil for three hours, cut open and spoon out the cooked fillings.

Auld Scotland wants
nae skinking ware
That jaups in luggies;
But, if ye wish her
gratefu' prayer,
Gie her a Haggis!

ROBERT BURNS

Oats have been at the heart of the daily Scottish diet since medieval times. They are used in the making of many classic Scottish dishes – porridge, oatcakes, bannocks, skirlie, haggis and mealy pudding, to name but a few. The really good news is that oats are good for you – they lower blood pressure, absorb toxins and clean artery walls, as well as being responsible for the release of testosterone which increases the sex drive in women and men, hence the popular Scottish phrase, 'get your oats'.

Everyone knows the world's best steak comes from cows raised in Aberdeenshire or Angus, and cuts from the **Aberdeen-Angus** breed are a major source of export income for the economy. The cows come in two colours – black or red – and can reach up to a staggering weight of 1,300 pounds at maturity. Imagine that on your plate!

What butter and whisky will not cure, there is no cure for.

SCOTTISH PROVERB

A Scottish dessert, traditionally enjoyed as a treat around harvest time when all the hard work was done, **cranachan** is basically just an excuse to mix together all your favourite guilty pleasures – whisky, honey and whipped cream along with a few fresh raspberries and toasted oats. An authentic way of serving this dish is to bring all the ingredients out separately and let your guests assemble their own! Just don't be the last to go – there'll be no whisky, cream or honey left!

Rumbledethumps is not just a beautiful word; it is also a beautiful Scottish dish not too dissimilar to England's bubble and squeak or Ireland's colcannon. The word itself evokes the concept of 'mashing' and the dish calls for exactly that. Potato, cabbage and onion (or pretty much any leftovers from a previous meal) are all rumbledethumped together and served either as a main or as a side dish. Happy rumbledethumping!

Soft and crumbly textured, **Edinburgh rock** is nothing like its name suggests. Apart from the Edinburgh part, that is. Not to be confused with its much harder English cousin, Blackpool rock, this colourful rock type is made of the usual suspects – sugar, sugar and more sugar – but with an added splash of cream of tartar.

The tasty all-butter biscuit known throughout the land as '**shortbread**' originated in Scotland and the country's most beloved brand, Walkers, is Scotland's biggest exporter of food, with shortbread being their number one best-selling product. Currently enjoying a renaissance, Walkers saw a 70 per cent increase in shortbread profits in 2013. Owner of the company, Mr Walker, backed up their success with the slogan: 'Shortbread is a traditional Scottish product. It is never in fashion. It is never out of fashion.' Hear! Hear!

The bright-orange, number-one-selling soft drink in Scotland, **Barr's Irn-Bru**, is popularly known as 'Scotland's other national drink' (whisky, of course, being the original). In 2011, over 200 million litres were sold – that's ten cans for every man, woman and child in the UK. Bottoms up!

In many ways, the **deep-fried Mars Bar** defines Scotland in one chewy bite: part myth, part fantasy, part tongue-in-cheek fun. With over 1,200 calories per bar, this treat has just enjoyed its twentieth birthday, having been invented in a fish and chip bar in Stonehaven in the 1990s. Up to 150 deep-fried Mars Bars are still sold every week at the shop, with 70 per cent being sold to inquisitive visitors to the town.

My home could be anywhere but I love Glasgow.

KELLY MACDONALD

MAPPING
THE NATION

OUR WEATHER
AND GEOGRAPHY

Scotland's **longest freshwater river**, the Tay, is 188 kilometres (117 miles) long and originates in western Scotland, 720 metres (2,362 feet) above sea level on the slopes of Ben Lui, before flowing in an easterly direction across the Highlands, all the way to the North Sea. At its deepest point the river reaches down 149 metres (490 feet) below its surface.

Scotland has **790 islands**, of which only about a hundred or so are inhabited by humans. The most remote island is Fair Isle, which lies alone between the Orkney Islands to the south-west and the mainland of Shetland to the north-east. The island of Unst in the Shetlands is the northernmost inhabited island – home to around 600 people.

The Scots are steadfast
– not their clime.

THOMAS CRAWFORD

Scotland's **lowest point** is the bed of Loch Morar, which sits 300 metres (987 feet) below sea level. Locals around Loch Morar believe a Nessie-like creature lives there – they call it Morag.

Ben Nevis (Gaelic for 'venomous mountain') resides in the Grampian mountain range and, at 1,334 metres (4,409 feet), is the **highest peak** in the British Isles. The famous peak of this iconic mountain is the result of the collapsed dome of a volcano that imploded many millions of years ago. The poet John Keats climbed the mountain in 1818 and compared the ascent to 'mounting ten St Paul's Cathedrals without the convenience of a staircase'.

This is my country,
The land that begat me.

ALEXANDER GRAY

The island of Tiree in the Hebrides
received a total of 329 hours of sunshine
in May 1946 and May 1975. This is the
highest number of **sunshine hours**
ever recorded in one month in Scotland,
an average of 10.6 hours a day.

Scotland, when compared to the rest of Europe, has a relatively low **population density** – sixty-five people per square kilometre. Glasgow is the most populated city in the country, with around 600,000 people. In 2013 the island of Sanda, the least populated island off Scotland at the time (population: one) became closed off to the public after a Swiss millionaire bought the entire island for £2.5 million.

Scottish by birth,
British by law,
Highlander by the
grace of God.

ANONYMOUS

The Butt of Lewis, the northernmost point in the Outer Hebrides (next stop Canada!), is the **windiest place** in the United Kingdom. Great name for a great fact.

The **lowest temperature** in Scotland ever recorded was −27.2 °C (17 °F) in Braemar on 10 January 1982. That will freeze your neeps and tatties off, for sure! The **highest temperature** on record was a sweltering (well, for Scotland anyway) 32.9 °C (91.2 °F) in Greycook, in the Scottish Borders, on 9 August 2003.

I 'scotched, not killed' the
Scotchman in my blood,
And love the land of
mountain and of flood.

LORD BYRON

THE OBJECTS
OF OUR
DESIRE

ICONIC OBJECTS AND
FAMOUS INVENTIONS

Ranked number forty-four in the BBC's Greatest Ever Britons, we have a lot to thank John Logie Baird for. For one thing, he kindly invented the world's first **television**. The contribution in this field was not his alone, as many other inventors helped along the way, but it was Logie Baird who was the first to transmit a moving image. Not everything he invented turned to gold though. One of his many failed experiments occurred when he tried to create diamonds by heating graphite, and ended up shorting out Glasgow's entire electricity supply!

Forget Sherlock Holmes. Next time you see someone caught red-handed for thieving, give two thumbs up to Ayrshire physician, missionary and scientist Henry Faulds – he introduced **fingerprinting** to forensic science in 1880. The process has been used to identify criminals who left their mark behind at a crime scene, a fingerprint being unique to every human being on the planet, and brought the collection of forensic evidence into the modern world. Also, without Henry Faulds, there might have been no *CSI: Crime Scene Investigation*.

Thomas Telford has a nickname that most men would envy – the 'Colossus of Roads'! He is Scotland's most famous builder of **roads, canals and bridges**. We may take many of Telford's works – including around a thousand new bridges and over nine hundred miles of new roads in Scotland alone – for granted now, but if he hadn't engineered such ingenious roads and bridges, then travelling from A to B would be even more laborious than it is now.

In Scotland, everybody knows the 'water of life' is definitely not of the plain H_2O variety. **Scotch whiskies** are beloved and drunk in equal measure by millions of people around the world. Scotland has internationally protected the word 'Scotch', which means that only a whisky from Scotland can 'officially' bear the name. The earliest record of distilling whisky in Scotland dates back to 1494, and in 2011 Scotch whisky global sales were worth £4.5 billion!

Speed bonnie boat like
a bird on the wing,
Onward! the sailors cry;
Carry the lad that's
born to be king
Over the sea to Skye.

HAROLD BOULTON

Nobel Prize-winning biologist, pharmacologist and botanist, Alexander Fleming, discovered penicillin in 1928. **Penicillin** stops the growth of disease-causing microbes and has been labelled the world's first miracle drug. Fleming also discovered **lysosomes**, which carry out waste disposal within cells.

In 1996, **Dolly the sheep** became the first cloned mammal to be created from an adult cell… and the first ever celebrity sheep. It was the hard work and dedication of the biotechnology scientists at the Roslin Institute in Edinburgh that led to this monumental world first.

Next time you look down a **microscope**, give proud thanks to Robert Brown. This Scottish scientist's greatest contributions to the world were the pioneering of the microscope and the detailed discovery in 1831 of something very small, but incredibly important – the cell nucleus. A nucleus contains a living cell's genetic material.

I would rather have a Scot come from Scotland to govern the people of this kingdom well and justly than that you should govern them ill in the sight of all the world.

LOUIS IX, TO HIS SON

The kilt is a knee-length tartan garment worn as part of traditional Highland dress that dates back to the sixteenth century. The original meaning of the Scots word 'kilt' was 'to tuck up the clothes around the body'. A kilt is traditionally accessorised with an Argyll jacket, a sporran, hose and ghillie brogues, and a skean-dhu… with undergarments strictly optional.

For fans of modern mentalist Derren Brown, you may be interested to know that **hypnotism** has Scottish origins. Kinross-born surgeon James Braid – dubbed the 'father of modern hypnotism' – is considered the world's first genuine hypnotist (a term which he himself coined) after he put his first subject under his spell for the first time in 1841.

It was surely inevitable that the first person to invent the raincoat was Scottish. And so it was that inventor Charles Macintosh put two and two together – in this case, raindrops and rubberised fabric. **The Mackintosh**, as it became known, first went on sale in 1824 and not only gave the world a new fashion style, but also changed our outlook towards the weather, which suddenly seemed conquerable – no longer did we have to sit indoors and wait it out!

Bagpipes are the national instrument of Scotland and are a proud symbol of the nation's heritage, not least because they were once used to strike fear into the country's enemies. Despite only being capable of nine notes, bagpipes are exceptionally difficult to play.

Born in 1900, **Isobel Hogg Kerr Beattie** is regarded as the first female architect to work professionally in Scotland. After attending Edinburgh College of Art, Isobel worked for a local architectural firm, Jamieson and Arnott. She later became one of the first women to be certified by the Royal Institute of British Architects. She worked extensively on the beautiful Buccleuch Estates, which comprised four massive mansion houses, each one originally belonging to the well-to-do Buccleuch family.

Scotsmen are metaphysical and emotional, they are sceptical and mystical, they are romantic and ironic, they are cruel and tender, and full of mirth and despair.

WILLIAM DUNBAR

A LAW UNTO OURSELVES

OURSELVES

THE PECULIAR LAWS THAT KEEP US OUT OF TROUBLE!

Up until 2002, Scottish workers did not have the legal right to refuse to work on a Sunday, unlike shopworkers in England and Wales. This was an anomaly within UK employment law, but the Sunday Working Scotland Act 2003 put a stop to it.

A Scots pessimist is a man who feels badly when he feels good for fear he'll feel worse when he feels better.

SCOTTISH PROVERB

In Scotland, it is illegal for a boy under
the age of ten to see a naked mannequin.
(Heaven knows how this is enforced!)

Despite the British government slashing
45,000 laws from the statute book
in 2006, it is still, under the Salmon
Act 1986, illegal to 'handle salmon
in suspicious circumstances'.

It is illegal, under the Licensing Act 1872,
to be drunk on licensed premises,
e.g. a pub.

I always liked Scotland
as an idea, but now, as a
reality, I like it far better…

CHARLOTTE BRONTË

The Library Offences Act 1898
banned all gambling in libraries.
(There must have been a lot
of gambling in libraries!)

It's ill taking the breeks
aff a Hielandman.

WALTER SCOTT

Any Scot found wandering around the town of Carlisle, Cumbria, may be whipped or jailed. (A law passed after Scotland had returned Cumbria to the English crown in the twelfth century.)

In Scotland, the law obliges citizens to allow whoever knocks on their door to use their toilet, and refusal is punishable by death!

It is legal to kill a Scotsman within the city walls of York, but only if he is carrying a bow and arrow.

By order of Prerogativa Regis, 1322,
the head of any dead whale found
on the Scottish coast automatically
became the property of the king,
and the tail that of the queen.

Under the Tax Avoidance Schemes Regulations 2006, it is illegal not to tell the taxman anything you do not want him to know, but legal not to tell him information you do not mind him knowing. (Confused?)

Under the Wildlife and Countryside
Act 1981 it is illegal to eat mute
swan (it's a protected species) unless
you're the Queen of Great Britain.

Under the Licensing Act 1872, it is an
offence to be 'drunk in charge of a
carriage, horse, cow or steam engine,
whilst in possession of a loaded firearm.'
(Drunk in possession of a cow? Sounds fun.)

Twelve highlanders and a
bagpipe make a rebellion.

SCOTTISH PROVERB

THERE'S NO PLACE LIKE HOME

FAMOUS PLACES TO SEE AND THINGS TO DO

St Ninian's beach in the Shetland Islands, on a sunny day, wouldn't look out of place in the Caribbean. As one of the finest and largest sand tombolos in Europe (a tombolo is a bar of sand that joins an island to a mainland), St Ninian's has recently made it into a travel magazine's top ten 'best swims in the world'. Obviously, the water's freezing – it's still Scotland, after all – but this beach has to be seen to be believed!

Popularly known as the 'Scottish Pompeii', **Skara Brae** is one of Europe's most complete Neolithic dwellings and forms part of the Heart of Neolithic Orkney, a UNESCO World Heritage Site. Located on the Bay of Skaill, the largest island in the Orkney archipelago, Skara Brae consists of eight stone-built Neolithic houses. It was inhabited from *c.*3180 to *c.*2500 BC, making the site older than Stonehenge *and* the Great Pyramids.

Known as an '**Old Firm**' game, a Rangers v. Celtic match is the ultimate clash of Scottish heads, no matter whether it is played at Ibrox (Rangers), Parkhead (Celtic) or Hampden (the national stadium used for cup finals). Encapsulating a long history of fierce rivalry, this football clash is well worth the cost of the ticket and one of the fiercest sporting derbies in the country.

From the lone shieling
of the misty island
Mountains divide us,
and the waste of seas –
Yet still the blood is strong,
the heart is Highland,
And we in dreams
behold the Hebrides!

FROM 'CANADIAN BOAT SONG'

One of the most exhausting, but also exhilarating, expeditions to enjoy and endure in Scotland (if you have the stamina, of course) is walking the **West Highland Way** – a 154-kilometres (96-mile) trek that stretches from Milngavie, near Glasgow, all the way to Fort William at the foot of Ben Nevis in the north. En route you'll pass Loch Lomond, Rob Roy's hideout cave, Rannoch Moor and the amazing Glen Coe.

During the winter solstice, at the magical **Maeshowe tomb** (2750 BC) in Neolithic Orkney something mystical happens. During the shortest day of the year – usually 21 or 22 December – you'll be able to experience the final passing rays of the winter-solstice sun streaming down the tomb's passage and illuminating the central chamber. Even though modern experts are still unsure of the significance of what this meant for the architects of the cave, it certainly portrays them as enlightened astronomers who were way ahead of their time.

One of life's simplest pleasures is throwing a stone into water. Well, at **Mavis Grind**, a narrow neck on the Shetland mainland, you'll be able to take great pleasure in throwing a stone from the North Sea *into the Atlantic*. Mavis Grind is where the North Sea and the Atlantic almost, but don't quite, meet, making this one of the few places on earth where you can stand and drink in the two mighty expanses of water at the same time.

If Scotland had a national fish it would undoubtedly be the salmon. So why not go **salmon fishing** in that most Scottish of rivers, the Tweed, which flows eastwards through the Borders region? The best time to go is September, when you'll find the water bustling with migrating salmon stocks. The water will be freezing, so make sure you don't fall in.

Of all the small nations of this earth, perhaps only the Ancient Greeks surpass the Scots in their contribution to mankind.

WINSTON CHURCHILL

The classic Indian dish '**chicken tikka masala**' is actually said to have originated at the Shish Mahal in Gibson Street (since moved to Park Road), Glasgow. In 2009, Pakistani-born Glasgow MP Mohammad Sarwar tabled a motion in the House of Commons asking that parliament support a campaign for the city to be given European Union Protected Designation of Origin status for chicken tikka masala. The motion was sadly not chosen for debate. However, one in seven curries ordered in the UK is a chicken tikka masala, making it the most popular restaurant dish in the country.

Glasgow's beautiful Gothic cemetery, the
Necropolis, is home to 50,000 bodies
and mammoth monuments to the dead
and a few hundred weeping statues.
Located next door to Glasgow Cathedral
since 1832, this Victorian-era cemetery
is based on Paris's Père-Lachaise.

Scotland is the country above all others that I have seen, in which a man of imagination may carve out his own pleasures.

DOROTHY WORDSWORTH

The awe-inspiring site of the **Standing Stones in Callanish**, Outer Hebrides, may pre-date Stonehenge by as much as half a millennium. Put in place overlooking Loch Roag, on the Isle of Lewis, up to five thousand years ago, presumably for astrological purposes, the Druids who erected these fifty massive stone 'sentinels' must have had help from aliens. Or have been giants.

The **Antonine Wall**, which ran between the Firth of Forth in the east and the Firth of Clyde in the west, represented the northernmost frontier barrier to the Romans' attempts to include Scotland in their empire. Taking about twelve years to complete, construction started around AD 142 (around twenty years after the building of Hadrian's Wall). The wall was 63 kilometres (39 miles) long and 3 metres (9.8 feet) high, and surrounded by a deep ditch on the northern side. Any parts of the wall that remain are looked after by Historic Scotland with support from the UNESCO World Heritage Committee.

O ye'll tak' the high road,
and I'll tak' the low road,
And I'll be in
Scotland afore ye,
But me and my true love
will never meet again,
On the bonnie, bonnie
banks o' Loch Lomond.

ANONYMOUS

If you're interested in finding out more
about our books, find us on Facebook at
Summersdale Publishers and follow us
on Twitter at **@Summersdale**.

www.summersdale.com